Dear common flower, that grow'st beside the way,
Fringing the dusty road with harmless gold...

—JAMES RUSSELL LOWELL

DANDELION

celebrating the magical blossom

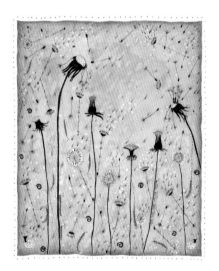

Amy S. Wilensky
Illustrations by **Yumi Heo**

COUNCIL OAK BOOKS

SAN FRANCISCO/TULSA

Saving the Dandelions

Growing up, I used to love to watch my father mow the lawn. I would sit on the front steps for hours as he wove back and forth, relishing the neat paths left in his wake, the reassuring hum of the mower, the unparalleled smell of freshly cut grass. Until one dark day, when I made a connection that was to forever mar my relationship with newly mowed lawns and with one cigar-smoking, baseball-capped mower in particular. After a class trip to a local farm where we had picked and then sautéed dandelion greens in the farmhouse kitchen, the flowers had taken on for me a newfound significance, and I could no longer stand by in silence while they were cut down before their time.

Thus began a nearly decade-long duel. My murderous father was determined to achieve the perfect suburban lawn, and I set out with equal determination on what would become my most infamous childhood mission:

to save the dandelions. Day after day, I attempted to interfere with his mowing, standing in his path, strewing my dolls across the grass, calling him into the house to answer nonexistent telephone calls. I spent hours showing my sister how to blow on the downy heads while spinning in circles so more and more seeds would take root. I picked bouquets and placed them around the house in little jars.

"They're weeds," my father explained.

"They're flowers," I shot back. "It's all in the way you look at things." My mother pretended to remain neutral, but the night she suggested we make a dandelion salad for dinner, I knew she was on my side.

It has been a long time since I last tried to stop anyone from mowing the dandelions. With age, I have succumbed perhaps to the adult aesthetic of immaculate lawns. I now know the technical difference between a weed and a flower. But come June, at first sight of those familiar yellow heads, I feel a twinge of nostalgia, a surge of joy. And I take secret pleasure in my knowledge that although my father still mows the lawn obsessively, and I have left him alone to do so, he will never really triumph over the persistent dandelion. Today when I pull into the driveway and happen to see him mowing, he waves and I smile without a twinge of anger. I take my comfort in the knowledge that the dandelion is not the only one whose roots run deep.

Food of the Gods

The most essential and arguably the least widely known fact about dandelions is this: they are amazingly good for you, from the blossoms to the leaves to the roots. Dandelions absorb many nutrients from the soil, in particular iron, vitamin A and vitamin C. Just one serving of dandelion greens contains 50 percent more vitamin C than a comparable serving of tomatoes, twice as much protein as eggplant, double the fiber of asparagus, as much iron as spinach and more potassium than bananas. Dandelions are nature's richest vegetable source of cancer-fighting beta-carotene, and the third richest source of vitamin A of all foods, after cod-liver oil and beef liver. They are also rich in vitamin D, calcium, magnesium, phosphorus, thiamine and riboflavin. Dandelion greens are increasingly available year round in the produce sections of supermarkets.

The nutritious properties of the jaunty dandelion are not a modern discovery. According to legend, Hecate fed Theseus a dish of dandelions each day for thirty days just before he was to fight the Marathonian Bull in the belief that the plant would endow him with strength and power.

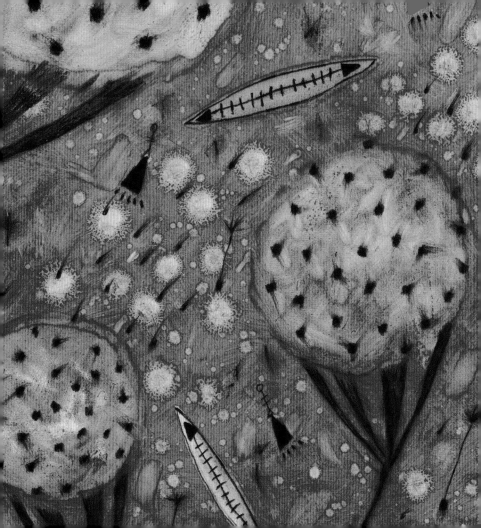

By Any Other Name

The aptly named dandelion (dandy lion!) has dounceens of aliases. Its botanical name is *Taraxacum officinale;* the genus name *Taraxacum* is derived from the Persian word for "bitter herb." The Latin name, in which the roots of the modern English are obvious, is *dens leonis,* and, likewise, the Greek name is *leontodon.* However, this versatile plant has many other, more evocative, common and descriptive names, among them *dent de lion* ("tooth of the lion" in French), clearly derived from the Latin. This is most often attributed to the "toothed" shape of the leaves, although some say it is because the yellow petals resemble the gilded teeth of a heralded lion or because the roots are so very white, like a tooth. A fifteenth-century surgeon's report claims that the plant is as strong as a lion's tooth, which may also account for this nomenclature. Other less formal dandelion nick-names that have been passed down over the centuries include Blow-balls, Priest's Crown, Monk's Head, Telltime, Faceclock, Noor-head Clocks, Doonhead Clock, Cankerwort, Swine's Snout and Pissabed (for its diuretic effects).

Sautéed Dandelion Greens

This is perhaps the classic dandelion green preparation and is delicious served with roasted meats or as part of a vegetarian meal.

Serves 2-4

- 1 pound dandelion greens (no roots or blossoms), washed and dried
- 1 yellow onion, diced
- 2-4 garlic cloves, finely minced

- 2-4 garlic cloves, finely minced
- pinch cayenne pepper (optional)
- 3 tablespoons high-quality olive oil
- salt and pepper

Cut leaves into 2-inch pieces. Place in a pot with 1 cup of boiling water and cook until just tender and still bright green, not more than 10 minutes. Drain and set aside. Sauté the onion and garlic in the oil until just golden; add cayenne, salt and pepper. Add the greens to the pan with the onion and garlic mixture. Sauté for a few more minutes, until hot. Serve immediately with lemon wedges or grated Parmesan cheese, if desired.

Nature's Timepiece

Some young and saucy dandelions
Stood laughing in the sun;
They were brimming full of happiness,
And running o'er with fun.
At length they saw beside them
A dandelion old;
His form was bent and withered,
Gone were his locks of gold.
"Oh, oh!" they cried, "just see him;
Old greybeard, how d'ye do?
We'd hide our heads in the grasses,
If we were as bald as you."
But lo! When dawned the morning,
Up rose each tiny head,
Decked not with golden tresses,
But long grey locks instead.

—ANONYMOUS

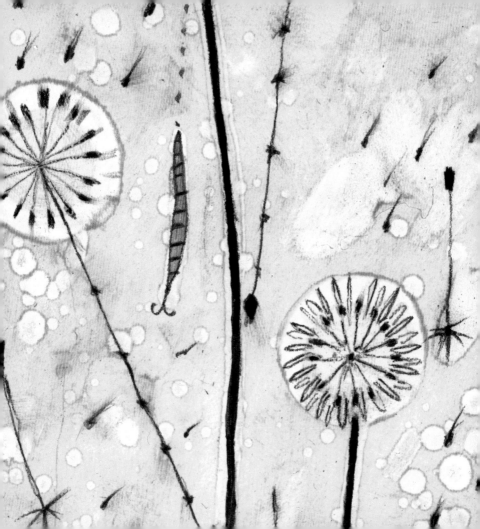

Dandelion Jelly

A delicious, healthful jelly, which is excellent served on toasted scones or biscuits. Makes a lovely gift decorated with fresh dandelion flowers.

2 cups dandelion blossoms
2 cups water
2¼ cups sugar
2 tablespoons powdered pectin
1 tablespoon lemon juice

Make sure the dandelion blossoms are clean and dry. Put them in a large pan with the water and bring to a boil; boil for 3 minutes. Strain the mixture and discard the blossoms. Add the pectin and lemon juice to the liquid. Bring to a boil again, and add the sugar. Boil for 3 minutes, stirring continuously. Pour into sterilized jelly jars and seal with paraffin or custom-made lid. Prepare a pan of boiling water and place jars in the water for 5 minutes. You should have 2½ cups of dandelion jelly.

Breath of Prophecy

Dandelions are the subjects of many superstitions and fanciful stories in cultures around the world. Some of the most enduring of these involve the blowing of the downy white head once the flower is past its prime, an act with which any child raised in the country can relate.

Your wish will come true if all of the seeds are blown off in one breath. If some do remain, that is the number of children you will have.

To find out how long you will live, blow once on a dandelion head. The number of seeds remaining is the number of years your life will hold.

To send a message to a loved one, concentrate on what you wish to say, and blow the seeds in the direction of your intended recipient. The seeds will carry your message to the one you love.

Dandelion seeds floating free in the wind represent gossip in the air. If a seed lands on you, you are the subject of the gossip.

The Magical Blossom

Many mystical powers have been attributed to the humble dandelion, probably due to its remarkable healing properties and versatility. For instance:

Bury whole dandelion flowers at the northwest corner of your home to bring favorable winds and weather.

Rub the white sap of the dandelion stem on warts to make them disappear.

Hold a dandelion flower in full bloom under your chin. If you see a yellow reflection, you like butter. Similarly, rub the yellow blossom onto your chin. If a yellow powder adheres, you like butter.

Send a child to search out the tallest dandelion he or she can find. The number of inches the stem measures is the number of inches the child will grow that year.

Make dandelion "coffee" from ground roasted roots and place a steaming cup by your bedside just before falling asleep. This will call the spirits of your choice to appear in your dreams.

The Silesians believed that dandelions picked on Midsummer Eve would ward off witches.

In Holland, it is believed that a Dutchman who eats a dandelion salad on Maundy Thursday (the Thursday before Easter) will remain healthy all year. ✳

Weed of the Poet

Its little Ether Hood Doth
Sit upon its Head—
The millinery supple
Of the sagacious God—

Till when it slip away
A nothing at a time—
And Dandelion's Drama
Expires in a stem.
—EMILY DICKINSON

Forgive me if I never visit. I am from the fields, you know, and while quite at home with the dandelion, make a sorry figure in the drawing room.
—EMILY DICKINSON, from a letter to her sister

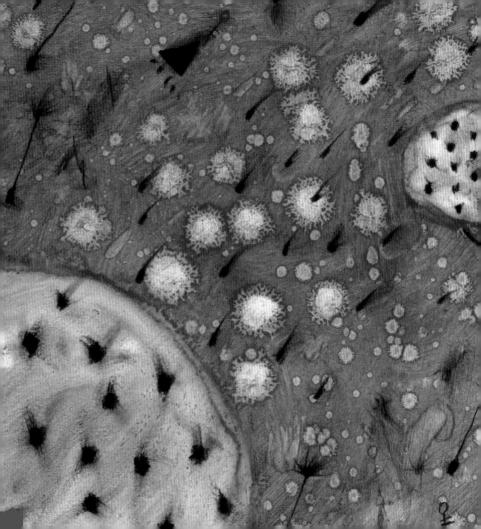

The Lion's Mane

Dandelions—like chamomile and marigolds—are a natural color enhancer for those with blonde or light brown hair. This all-natural hair rinse will give your hair a golden glow. (Be sure to rub a swab of the concoction on your inner arm before using it on your head to eliminate the unlikely possibility of an allergic reaction to dandelions.) This rinse mimics versions sold at expensive salons. It is easy to make and use, and may be decanted into a decorative bottle with a screw top and given as a gift. Try making handmade labels on dandelion paper and tying a green or yellow ribbon around the neck of the bottle. This recipe makes enough for one use.

To make:

Gather 3 cups tightly packed dandelion heads in full bloom. Place in a large pot and pour in cold water to cover. Boil for one hour (the liquid will reduce, but add more if it is boiling dry). Strain into a pitcher and let cool before pouring over damp, freshly washed hair. Wrap hair in a dark towel for at least half an hour, then rinse with clean water and dry.

Time's Durable Blossom

Although today they are oft maligned and considered by some unknowing observers to be little more than lawn pests, dandelions have an impressive heritage and have been highly valued for thousands of years. In earlier times, the dandelion was actually cultivated as a garden plant, a trend that is taking hold again today. The dandelion is thought to have originated in Asia about thirty million years ago, but it probably spread throughout the world well before the beginning of recorded history. Dandelion fossils have been found, testimony to its prehistoric roots. Legend tells us that the Minorcans survived on dandelions when a locust plague destroyed all of their crops, leaving only the hardy dandelions. And scholars have speculated that dandelion greens were among the bitter herbs consumed by ancient Hebrew people on the first Passovers, as the plant is common in Egypt and western Asia. The dandelion appears in the tenth-century journals of some Arabian physicians; by the sixteenth century, the British considered the dandelion an invaluable source of food and an essential herbal treatment. When the Puritans set out from England to settle in America, they brought the dandelion along with them for their gardens.

How did the dandelion survive for so long on voyages across the sea and through harsh winters in many parts of the world? The dandelion is an especially hardy perennial. Its roots remain alive all winter, even under cover of snow and ice. They grow and spread, and, come spring, new plants emerge, along with the plants from the previous year. When dandelion season draws to a close, the seeds float on wind currents; when they land, sometimes miles from their plant of origin, they germinate, meaning even more plants will emerge the following year. A typical dandelion possesses more than two hundred yellow florets with a seed attached to each. That gives it a lot of chances to reproduce.

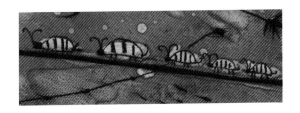

a Dandelion a Day

Dandelions are more than just good for you—many doctors, scientists and nutritionists consider them to be something of a miracle cure. Dandelions are considered an official remedy in most countries, and in China, where herbal medicine is a part of daily life, dandelion is one of the top six herbs in the Chinese herbal medicine chest. Whether consumed as part of your regular diet, or taken as a beverage or herbal supplement, dandelions can prevent or help cure liver diseases such as hepatitis and jaundice, improve your bowel function (relieving both constipation and diarrhea), lower your cholesterol, prevent or lower high blood pressure, work as a diuretic to help cleanse your system, dissolve kidney stones, prevent or help cure anemia, eliminate or reduce acid indigestion and gas and much, much more. When confronted with any of these ailments, first and foremost seek the advice of a practicing physician, but rest assured that there are no negative side effects associated with the use of dandelions as an herbal remedy. That's certainly more than can be said about most prescription medications!

Written on the Wind

The bright colors of dandelion petals and leaves are stunning in these one-of-a-kind sheets of handmade paper. Use your dandelion paper to make labels for other dandelion products, such as wine, jelly and hair rinse.

2-4 sheets poster-size paper,
   such as that used for sketching,
   or light newspaper pages,
   ripped into 1-inch squares
2 tablespoons white glue
2 cups water,
   plus extra if needed
food processor

iron
old screen(s), such as from a window
plastic tub filled with 3 inches water
bowl
food coloring (optional)
1 cup dandelion petals, dried
   and/or 1 cup dandelion leaves,
   dried and torn into small pieces

Cut the screen(s) into rectangles the size you wish your sheets of paper to be, approximately 6 x 8 inches. Make a bunch of these frames, as you will need one for each sheet of paper.

Put a handful of the paper scraps and ¼ cup water in the food processor. Process briefly. Continue to add scraps and water until you have a large mass. Add food coloring, if desired. Process the mass for 2 minutes. Add the glue to the water in the tub, then add the mixture from the food processor. Add the dandelion petals and/or greens to the tub. Mix thoroughly with your hands.

Scoop a screen frame to the bottom of the tub and lift very slowly until just above the water. Tilt gently to evenly distribute the mixture. Set above a bowl with the mixture-coated side facing up to let the water drain out. Then set the frame in the sun or under a lamp to dry thoroughly. When dry, carefully peel off the paper. Place the paper under a dishtowel or sheet of cotton fabric, and then iron the paper with a hot iron.

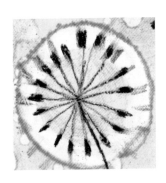

The Sensitive Plant

The dandelion has obvious connotations of health and vitality, radiance and strength. It has also been used as a potent symbol throughout history. Flemish and German painters used images of dandelions in representations of the crucifixion to portray the suffering of Christ. In other paintings, the dandelion was meant to convey coquetry or the sun. In mythology, dandelions symbolize faithfulness, grief, and bitterness. The traditional Victorian language of flowers used dandelions to symbolize the ancient oracles and the power to predict the future. Like all living things, the dandelion has been assigned astrological associations, as follows:

GENDER	Masculine
ELEMENT	Air
PLANET	Jupiter
DEITIES	Hecate, Belenos, Sun Gods

Good for What Ails You

Dandelion teas have traditionally been used to treat a number of ailments. Although none of these concoctions is meant to be used as a substitute for prescribed medications, they have all been used for thousands of years to great effect. Always consult a medical doctor when experiencing any of these conditions or symptoms, then proceed with preparing and imbibing the appropriate tea. In addition, any of these teas may simply be enjoyed, hot or chilled, as a refreshing beverage.

For biliousness and dropsy
Infuse 1 ounce of dandelion root in a pint of boiling water for 10 minutes. Decant, sweeten with honey and enjoy.

For a sluggish liver
Boil 2 ounces of dandelion root in 2 pints of water until reduced to 1 pint. Add 1 ounce of compound tincture of horseradish. Drink in small amounts.

For dizziness

In 3 pints of water, simmer 1 ounce dandelion root, 1 ounce black horehound herb, $\frac{1}{2}$ ounce sweet flag root and $\frac{1}{4}$ ounce mountain flax until you have 1$\frac{1}{2}$ pints liquid. Strain and drink after meals.

For gallstones

In 2 quarts of water, place 1 ounce dandelion root, 1 ounce parsley root, 1 ounce balm herb, $\frac{1}{2}$ ounce ginger root and $\frac{1}{2}$ ounce licorice root. Boil down to 1 quart of liquid, strain. Drink a glass every 2 hours.

For jaundice

Add to 3 pints of water, 1 ounce dandelion root, $\frac{1}{2}$ ounce ginger root, $\frac{1}{2}$ ounce caraway seeds, $\frac{1}{2}$ ounce cinnamon stick and $\frac{1}{4}$ ounce senna leaves. Boil until reduced to 1$\frac{1}{2}$ pints, strain, add $\frac{1}{2}$ pound sugar and bring to a boil again. Skim the surface of the liquid, set aside to cool and take in 1-teaspoon doses.

For liver and kidney ailments

In 1$\frac{1}{2}$ pints water place $\frac{1}{2}$ ounce dandelion root, 1 ounce broom tops and $\frac{1}{2}$ ounce juniper berries. Boil for 10 minutes, then strain and add a pinch of cayenne. Take 1 tablespoon 3 times a day.

Crown of Gold

> She fell into a softened remembrance of meadows, in old time, gleaming with buttercups, like so many inverted firmaments of golden stars; and how she had made chains of dandelion—stalks for youthful vowers of eternal constancy, dressed chiefly in nankeen; and how soon those fetters had withered and broken.
>
> —CHARLES DICKENS, *Dombey and Son*

Daisy chains are ordinary, old hat, common—dandelion chains are golden and glorious. Next time you find yourself lounging idly on a dotted lawn or field, gather a lapful of dandelions in full bloom, snapping off the stems close to the ground, making sure they are at least several inches long. Three-quarters of the way up each stem, close to the flower head, make an inch-long slit with your fingernail (or a pen knife, if you must). Then, insert the stem of one dandelion into the slit in the stem of another, and pull it through as far as you can. Continue until you reach your desired length—then crown yourself or a loved one with nature's own gold, or drop a sunny necklace over his or her head.

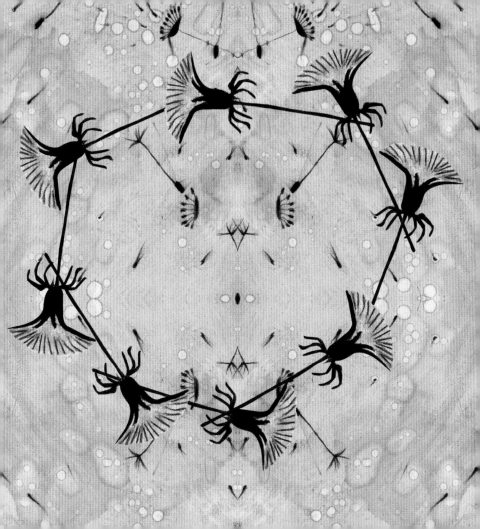

Dandelion Coffee

"I carefully washed the roots quite clean, without depriving them of the fine brown skin that covers them, which contains the aromatic flavour which so nearly resembles coffee.

I cut my roots into small pieces, and roasted them on an iron baking pan in the stone oven, until they were brown and crisp. I then ground and transferred a small cupful of powder to the coffee pot, pouring upon it scalding water, and boiling it for a few minutes briskly over the fire. The result was beyond my expectations. The coffee proved excellent—far superior to the common coffee we procured at the stores."

—SUSANNA MOODIE, *Roughing it in the Bush, or Life in Canada,* 1852

A modern version: Gather dandelion roots. Clean them well and let dry thoroughly for several hours, at least. When they are dry, roast them in an oven preheated to 350 degrees until they are a rich, brown color. Grind in a coffee grinder and prepare as you would regular coffee, using about 1 teaspoon powder for 1 cup water. Delicious!

Seize the Dandelion

Dandelion this,
A college youth that flashes for a day
All gold; anon he doffs his gaudy suit,
Touch'd by the magic hand of some
Grave Bishop,
And all at once, by commutation strange,
Becomes a Reverend Divine.
—JAMES HURDIS, *The Village Curate*, 1788

With locks of gold today;
To-morrow, silver-grey;
Then blossom-bald. Behold,
O man, thy fortune told!
—JOHN B. TABB, Nineteenth-Century Poet

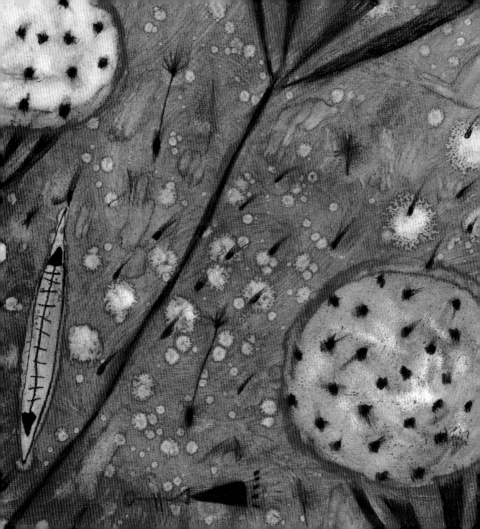

Dandelion Wine

Dandelion wine. The words were summer on the tongue.
—RAY BRADBURY, *Dandelion Wine*

2 quarts dandelion flowers,
 no greens attached

3 pounds sugar

2 lemons

2 oranges

1 gallon boiling water

½ ounce yeast

1 slice stale bread, toasted

Pick the dandelion flowers (heads only) on a sunny day when the flowers are open. Wash carefully and place in a large bowl. Slice lemons and oranges as thinly as possible and place in bowl with flowers. Pour boiling water into bowl and stir. Cover the bowl tightly and let sit for 10 days. Then strain the liquid into a clean bowl and add 3 pounds sugar. Sprinkle the yeast onto a piece of toast and float on top of the mixture. Cover and let sit for 3 more days. Then remove the toast and strain again. Pour into a sterilized bottle, cork and enjoy, either new or after the wine has aged. This delicate pale yellow wine is summer incarnate.

Harbingers of Warmth

Simple and fresh and fair from winter's close emerging,
As if no artifice of fashion, business, politics, had ever
been,
Forth from its sunny nook of shelter'd grass
—innocent, golden, calm as the dawn,
The spring's first dandelion shows its trustful face.
—WALT WHITMAN, 1888

The dandelions and buttercups
Gild all the lawn; the drowsy bee
Stumbles among the clover tops,
And summer sweetens all to me.
—JAMES RUSSELL LOWELL, 1869

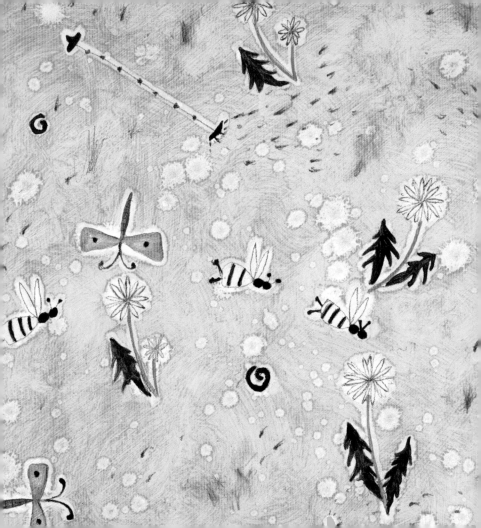

Dandelion Blossom Fritters, Italian Style

Although you may have enjoyed zucchini blossoms prepared this way, dandelion blossoms are just as well suited to the dish and have long been a treat in Mediterranean countries.

Serves 4

For fritter batter:

2 egg yolks

2/3 cup milk

2 cups flour

1/2 teaspoon salt

1 tablespoon melted butter

2 tablespoons lemon juice

2 egg whites, beaten until stiff

2 cups dandelion buds, gathered before flowers have opened, washed and dried

2 cups vegetable oil

Make fritter batter by whisking first six ingredients together until just combined and then folding in egg whites. Do not overmix. Dip blossoms in batter and then fry in hot oil until golden brown. Serve with lemon wedges and grated Parmesan cheese.

EXERCISE CAUTION AND BE SURE TO CONSULT A RELIABLE GUIDE TO EDIBLE WILD
PLANTS BEFORE PICKING AND EATING ANY PLANT IN THE WILD.

Council Oak Books, LLC
1290 Chestnut Street, Ste. 2, San Francisco, CA 94109
1350 E. 15th Street, Tulsa, OK 74120

Book and jacket design by Shannon Laskey

ISBN 1-57178-093-9
First edition / First printing.
Printed in South Korea.
00 01 02 03 04 05 06   5 4 3 2 1

"Gerald!
Oh, my word, he came out like a dandelion in the sun!
He's a whole saturnalia in himself,
once he is roused."
—D. H. Lawrence, *Women in Love*